FROM THE

… your birthch…
mation about y…
like to know w…
given birthchart… …likely reoccur approximately
every 26,000 years; therefore, your astrological twin
could possibly be born 26,000 years from now. So
for now, in this lifetime, you are absolutely unique!

Many people go through life as one-dimensional
persons because they have not discovered the
muti-dimensional nature with which they were
born. Your birth chart is a record of the truth about
you, and when analyzed by a competent astrologer,
your chart will reveal your unique depth; multi-tal-
ents; and potentials for career, money, love, success, health, family, spirituality, and more.

You can learn from your own birth chart how to
best handle problems, make maximum use of your
strengths, overcome your weaknesses, and deal
with life more effectively, thus ensuring your own
happiness and success.

If you are a parent and have your children's birth
charts, you are better equipped to provide wise
counsel because you have extensive cosmic information about them as unique beings. You can also
learn how to strengthen friendships, marriages,
and business partnerships when you have knowledge of other people's charts.

About the Author

William Hewitt has been practicing astrology professionally, as an avocation, since early 1974. He is a member of the American Federation of Astrologers and specializes in natal charts and interpretation. Hewitt has also been a professional clinical hypnotist since 1972. He has his own practice in Colorado where he resides. A member of the National Writers Club, Hewitt lectures on various subjects including astrology, hypnosis, psychic phenomena, mind control, and other areas. He is the author of *Hypnosis*, *Beyond Hypnosis*, and *Tea Leaf Reading*.

To Write to the Author

If you wish to contact the authoror would like more information about this book, please write to the author in care of Llewellyn Worldwide and we will forward your request. Both the author and publisher appreciate hearing from you and learning of your enjoyment of this book and how it has helped you. Llewellyn Worldwide cannot guarantee that every letter written to the author can be answered, but all will be forwarded. Please write to:

William W. Hewitt
c/o Llewellyn Worldwide
P.O. Box 64383-351, St. Paul, MN 55164-0383, U.S.A.

**Please enclose a self-addressed, stamped envelope for reply,
or $1.00 to cover costs.
If outside the U.S.A., enclose international postal reply coupon.**

Free Catalog from Llewellyn

For more than 90 years Llewellyn has brought its readers knowledge in the fields of metaphysics and human potential. Learn aboutr the newest books in spiritual guidance, natural healing, astrology, occult philosophy and more. Enjoy book reviews, new age articles, a calendar of events, plus current advertised products and services. To get your free copy of *Llewellyn New Worlds of Mind and Spirit*, send your name and address to:

Llewellyn's New Worlds of Mind and Spirit
P.O. Box 64383-351, St. Paul, MN 55164-0383, U.S.A.

LLEWELLYN'S VANGUARD SERIES

The Truth About

POWER IN YOUR BIRTHCHART

by William Hewitt

1994
Llewellyn Publications
St. Paul, MN 55164-0383, U.S.A.

FIRST EDITION
First Printing, 1994

International Standard Book Number:
1-56718-351-4

LLEWELLYN PUBLICATIONS
A Division of Llewellyn Worldwide, Ltd.
PO Box 64383, St. Paul, MN 55164-0383

Other Books by William Hewitt

The Art of Self Talk
Astrology for Beginners
Beyond Hypnosis
Bridges to Success & Fulfillment
Hypnosis (originally titled *Daydream Your Way to Success*)
Tea Leaf Reading

Llewellyn Publications is the oldest publisher of New Age Sciences in the Western Hemisphere. This book is one of a series of introductory explorations of each of the many fascinating dimensions of New Age Science—each important to a new understanding of Body and Soul, Mind and Spirit, of Nature and Humanity's place in the world, and the vast unexplored regions of Microcosm and Macrocosm.

Please write for a full list of publications.

THE POWER OF SELF KNOWLEDGE

Knowledge is power. The more you know about a subject, the greater power you have to deal effectively with that subject. For example, if you graduated from a technical school on automobile mechanics you would have considerable power (knowledge) to deal effectively with any malfunction in an automobile. In other words, you could fix whatever went wrong with an automobile.

The same is true with everything in life that you need to deal with—the more you know, the more power you have to effectively handle a given situation.

You can gain this power (knowledge) from many sources. Some of the most obvious sources are; experience, schools, books, consulting with experts.

The single most important subject you will ever have to deal with in life is YOURSELF, and one of the most powerful sources of knowledge about yourself is a source you may never have thought of, or perhaps never even heard of. That source is your natal astrological BIRTHCHART.

Your birthchart can show virtually everything about yourself from cradle to grave: your strengths, your weaknesses, potentials, possible problems, possible good fortunes, family factors, love possibilities, career potentials and possibilities, health matters, and hundreds of other factors in your life.

From your birthchart there are methods to look into your future at specific times and assess the choices and probabilities that you will have at those times. Thus you have a powerful tool for mapping your life.

Your birthchart is a powerhouse of information about you. Armed with this knowledge, you have the power to make better decisions and choices so you can direct your life in the manner that you want. No longer would you be subject to the whims of chance—instead you would call your own shots, eliminating those whims of chance.

If you are a parent think how much power you would have to help your children if you knew virtually everything about their potentials and probabilities while they were still young. If your child's birthchart showed a strong interest and natural ability in mechanics, sciences, and engineering, you would encourage the child in those things and would not try to groom him/her to take over the family insurance business. You could help all of your children find their niche in life with the greatest probability of success.

You would be able to wisely counsel your children at every step in their life because you would have extensive knowledge gleaned from their birthcharts. And, as they grew older, you could introduce them to their birthcharts so they could start making decisions based on their own self-knowledge.

For yourself, you can learn from your own birthchart how you can best handle problems, make maximum use of your strengths, overcome your weaknesses, and deal with life more effectively, thus ensuring your own happiness and success.

With birthchart information, spouses are able to better understand their mate and take actions to create a solid, successful marriage.

Does all this sound like a miracle or too good to be true? Well, it is neither. Your birthchart is given to you as a birthright the moment you are born to serve as a map for you to follow as you travel through life. It is, however, up to you to obtain the chart and glean the information from it. Your Creator gives you life and provides the parameters for your birthchart, but it is up to you to actually live the life and use the parameters (birthchart map) if you choose to do so.

Tremendous power is given to each of us at birth. To exercise that power to our best advantage we need to know more about ourselves and that power. Our birthchart is the place to look for answers and guidance so we can make the best choices for our own benefit, happiness, and success.

Exactly what is a birthchart and how do we use it? The balance of this booklet explores the answer to this question.

THE BIRTHCHART

The birthchart is a map that shows the exact placement of the Sun, Moon, and eight planets (Mercury, Venus, Mars, Saturn, Jupiter, Uranus, Neptune, and Pluto) at a person's moment of birth in relationship to the location on Earth where the birth occurred. The reason these planetary placements are important will be discussed shortly.

No two people can have the same birthchart unless they are born in the same place at the same time. Even twins do not have identical birthcharts, though they are born in the same place, because there is a time lapse between the births, usually 20 minutes to an hour or so. Sometimes the time between births may be within 5 minutes or so. True, twins have *almost* identical birthcharts, but even one minute difference in birthtime results in subtle differences between the birthcharts.

Mathematically, any given birthchart can reoccur exactly every 26,000 years. Therefore, your astrological twin could possibly be born 26,000 years from now. So for now, in this lifetime, you are absolutely unique. There is no one else exactly like you.

This is why the horoscope columns in newspapers and magazines do not work except in a general way. These horoscope readings are for Sun Signs only, of which there are only twelve (Aries, Taurus, Gemini, Cancer, Leo, Virgo, Libra, Scorpio, Sagittarius, Capricorn, Aquarius, and Pisces). There are obviously more than twelve kinds of people in the world. I just pointed out that everyone is unique. Therefore, if there are 2 billion people in the world, it would take 2 billion birthcharts to properly give an accurate birthchart interpretation for each person. Sun Signs are a significant part of the birthchart interpretation to be sure, but not the whole story by a long shot.

So up to this point we know the following: You are unique and the accurate information concerning you can be gleaned from your astrological birthchart.

Now let's examine a birthchart and discuss it in general, non-technical terms. There is no intention here to teach you the specifics of how a chart is created nor to teach you 100% of what you need to know about birthchart interpretation. This is an overview of natal birthcharts and of the power they furnish so you can live better. To learn more about astrology and how to obtain your birthchart and interpretation, refer to the Appendix at the end of this booklet.

Figure One on next page is an astrological birthchart that shows the placement of the Sun, Moon, and planets at the *moment* I was born in relation to the point on earth *where* I was born (Toledo, Ohio). I am showing you this now just to familiarize you with the general appearance of a birthchart. I say "general appearance" because there are a variety of styles of birthcharts, and some show a great deal more astrological information than shown here. Figure One is a "bare bones" chart, which is sufficient in this booklet because we are not going to be concerned with the many intricate details of creating a chart and interpreting a chart.

We will discuss Figure One in more detail shortly. Keep in mind that the purpose of this booklet is to make you aware of the power in a birthchart and not to teach you to be an astrologer. Books referred to at the end of this booklet can give you a greater understanding of astrology.

First we need to look at the big picture of astrology and the philosophy of astrology so you can better understand the importance and power of a birthchart.

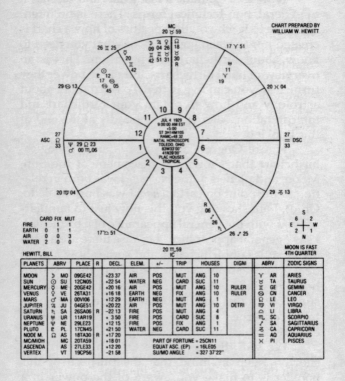

Figure 1
Natal Horoscope Chart

THE BIG PICTURE

The intent at this point is to give you a broad, general concept of natal astrology. By the end of this booklet you should know the what, why, and how of astrology at a basic, pre-beginners level.

"What is your Sun Sign?" is one of the most commonly asked questions between two people who are trying to get to know each other. Astrology fascinates people—they yearn to know how the heavens relate to their lives. Yet very few people have any real knowledge or understanding of astrology. To most people, astrology consists of those brief horoscope columns that appear in many newspapers and magazines. Those columns are fun, but they have little real use; they don't begin to touch on what astrology and horoscopes are all about.

Astrology is as old as measured time. There are probably as many different approaches to this fascinating subject as there are astrologers in the world today. In general, astrology embraces the idea that there is a connection between the heavens and Earth—that the heavens and Earth are united, interpenetrating, and sharing a common space and time. The great cosmic events happening beyond Earth (eclipses, planetary line-ups, etc.) do not cause events to occur on Earth but rather reflect the events happening on Earth. In other words, there is no cause in the heavens and then an effect here on Earth. Planetary events are not causing events here on Earth. Rather, both planetary and earthly events happen simultaneously and are mutually reflective. Neither is the cause of the other. Both are the product of the moment—one acted out in the heavens above, the other here on the Earth below.

There is only one grand drama. The great drama enacted in the sky is also acted out, in exact detail, here on Earth the same moment. Earth is part of the cosmos and shares in that cosmic moment. All major cosmic events are interactive; that is, they represent an activity also taking place within ourself, our consciousness, and in our daily lives.

Astrology is a study of heavenly cycles and cosmic events as they are reflected here in our earthly environment and vice versa. The movements and cycles of the planets form a huge cosmic clock that ticks off time and events—past, present, and future. The cosmic patterns revealed in the rhythmic motions of the planets shed light on the seeming helter-skelter of everyday life. It is easy to lose track of our direction in life due to the commotion of daily living. However, by studying our cosmic clock (astrology), we have a tool to give us better control and to see the order of things in what appears to be disorder at times.

Astrology is a study of the cycles of the Moon and planets and the Sun and their inter-relationships. There is not much in the heavens that is not cyclical—happening over and over. It is this repeating pattern that enables us to recognize heavenly events.

The Moon goes through four phases every 29 and ½ days: first quarter (New Moon); second quarter; third quarter (Full Moon); and fourth quarter. This waxing and waning of the Moon continues endlessly in an absolutely predictable pattern.

The Sun returns to the solstice and equinox points (spring, summer, autumn, and winter) predictably year after year.

Each planet has its own unique fixed orbit around the Sun. The planets, Moon, and Sun have predictable, repeating relationships to each other in space. All of these are circles or cycles. Astrology is a study of those events where there is a return or cycling.

The cosmos is a vast clock—wheels within wheels within wheels to which we all respond. A cosmic dance that performs endlessly.

A birthchart is a time-slice of this vast cosmic performance. The clock is stopped, in a manner of speaking. This is why the date, time, and place of birth are important. The moment of birth is a significant moment to stop the clock and examine the cosmic arrangement. Any important event is worth a cosmic snapshot. Some important dates are: birth of self, marriage, birth of children, etc. Any moment in time that a person considers significant is an event worthy of having a horoscope chart cast.

By studying the planetary arrangement for a given moment, the astrologer can gain an accurate picture of what has happened on Earth at that moment. This is what astrology is all about. This may sound like science fiction to you at this point, but believe me, it is very real. Astrology works! People who have had a chart cast and interpreted by a competent astrologer know that it is real.

The analysis of these important moments is very complex. The mathematics needed to erect a horoscope chart is tedious and time-consuming. The best way to erect a chart is to use a computer.

Astrology helps us to see ourself and life in a greater perspective—the big picture. Astrology also provides very specific information to help us direct the events in our life with greater success.

The more you learn about astrology, the more you will be concerned with cycles. Not only with the planetary cycles but also how these cycles show up in everyday life. The point of studying these cosmic cycles is to gain insight into how they appear in our lives here on Earth.

All of us notice some recurrence or cycling effects in our lives—certain habits, problems, and joys seem to occur to us over and over. These are the day-to-day or practical signs of the existence of cycles and our consciousness of them. Married people tend to be particularly aware of cycles since, in the ebb and flow of a very close relationship, we notice how we alternately have times of greater and less closeness. We come together and we drift apart, again and again.

Astrology offers a new way of organizing the events in our life—a way of seeing and understanding them. Astrology provides a way of understanding our experience. Learning to notice and take advantage of the cycles in our life can lead to an enhanced ability to handle the problems life presents. When we understand how cycles repeat themselves and how they work, we are prepared to get the most out of each phase of that cycle. Astrologers study, on the practical level, the endless ebbing and flowing—coming and going—of these cycles in our lives. One common misperception regarding astrologers is that they have their heads in the clouds. It is true that we have one eye to the heavens, but, most of all, we are concerned with the here and the now—with everyday events. We have learned to notice cycles and they fascinate us. We study these cycles with great attention. Our interest in the heavens springs from our experience here on Earth with the endless cycles and events surrounding us, into which each of us is born and must live.

Now I want to introduce you to some of the terms and tools of astrology. Keep in mind that the end result of astrology is to provide a tool that enables you to understand and live life better.

ASTROLOGICAL TERMS

The focus of this booklet is natal astrology and the power in the birthchart. The primary purpose of natal astrology is to construct a birthchart based on specific birth data and then to interpret the meanings in the chart in order to ascertain important information about the person whose birth data was used. Thus the birthchart is the principal tool for natal astrology.

The birthchart is called by various other names also: horoscope chart; natal chart; natal horoscope; chart wheel; radix wheel or chart; etc. Figure One is a birthchart. (see page 6)

At this point I don't expect you to understand Figure One. It is probably just a confusing jumble of abbreviations, symbols, and numbers. We will be referring back to Figure One a few times to explain parts of it. For now, I just want you to know what a birthchart looks like.

A birthchart consists of a series of mathematical calculations for the birth moment of a person. These calculations include the positions for the Sun, Moon, and eight planets in the Zodiac for the moment selected, plus several other sensitive points. This information is arranged in a CHART WHEEL form as shown in Figure One for the birth moment. Some of the main features of such a layout are:

Chart Wheel: The wheel is a 360 degree picture of the heavens at the time of the birth moment. The top of the chart is commonly called the MC or MIDHEAVEN. At the extreme left-hand side of the wheel is the ASCENDANT (ASC), often also called the RISING SIGN which is that part of the Zodiac that is on the horizon (rising) at the birth moment. The DESCENDANT (DSC) is on the right-hand side of the chart; this is the part of the Zodiac that is setting. The PLANETS are placed around the wheel where they appear in the Zodiac in the sky at the birth moment.

In Figure One, the planets and Zodiac Signs are shown by their 2-letter abbreviations and symbols as follows:

Zodiac Signs	Abbr.	Glyphs	Planets	Abbr.	Glyphs
Aries	AR	♈	Sun	SU	☉
Taurus	TA	♉	Moon	MO	☽
Gemini	GE	♊	Mercury	ME	☿
Cancer	CN	♋	Venus	VE	♀
Leo	LE	♌	Mars	MA	♂
Virgo	VI	♍	Jupiter	JU	♃
Libra	LI	♎	Saturn	SA	♄
Scorpio	SC	♏	Uranus	UR	♅
Sagittarius	SA	♐	Neptune	NE	♆
Capricorn	CP	♑	Pluto	PL	♇
Aquarius	AQ	♒			
Pisces	PI	♓			

Quite often the birthchart will use special symbols instead of the 2-letter abbreviations (as in Figure One). These special symbols are called glyphs. The GLYPHS are part of the special language of astrology. You will learn more about these if you choose to study astrology in more depth.

Planetary Positions: The planets are placed around the wheel in their Zodiac positions. The Zodiac is a convenient way to measure where a given planet is in the sky. The Zodiac stretches through all 360 degrees of the sky and is divided into the familiar 12 signs (Aries, Taurus, Gemini, etc.) of 30 degrees each. Planetary positions are measured within the Signs by degrees and minutes. For example, my Moon (at birth) is in the Sign Gemini (3rd sign) and in the 9th degree of Gemini, 42 minutes. My Moon is at 9 degrees and 42 minutes of the Sign Gemini. You can see this in Figure One. Look at the 10th house (top of chart in the pie-slice numbered 10). You will see the abbreviation MO with numbers 09 GE 42 below it. The "GE" is the abbreviation for the Zodiac Sign Gemini. The 09 and 42 tell the degrees and minutes of Gemini where the Moon was located when I was born.

House Cusps: Most astrologers divide the Zodiac into 12 sections or HOUSES according to a system. There are a number of house systems used by astrologers. Proponents of a particular house system often feel very deeply that their method of dividing the heavens is the most significant and that others are less meaningful.

    To better understand the next paragraph, you need to know what a house cusp is. The word "cusp" is the name of the lines in the chart that mark the beginning of a house. The houses are those 12 pie-shaped wedges in Figure One. The natal chart is read counterclockwise starting with the Ascendant (labeled ASC at the left side of Figure One), which is the horizontal line between the 12th and 1st house. Hence, the cusp of the 1st house is also the ASCENDANT.

    Most systems agree that the Ascendant marks the first house cusp, the Descendant marks the 7th, the Midheaven marks the 10th, and the NADIR marks the 4th house cusp. Look at the chart: wheel in Figure One and notice how it is divided into 12 sections or houses. The 1st house cusp is on the extreme left-hand side of the wheel and the 10th house cusp is on the top. The 7th-hand 4th houses are simply opposite the 1st and 10th houses. The remaining house cusps (2nd, 3rd, 5th, 6th, 8th, 9th, 11th, 12th) are called the intermediate house cusps because they are intermediate between the primary cusps (1st, 4th, 7th, and 10th). It is these intermediate cusps that differ (in general) from one house system to another.

I'm sure all this sounds confusing, and it is. It confused me when I was a beginner. Just let it rest lightly on your mind. It will clear up as we go on. For now, I just want to give you some notion of what house cusps and house systems are. The most popular house systems in use today are the PLACIDIAN and KOCH systems. The Placidian House System is used in Figure One. Simplistically, Placidian merely refers to a specific mathematical approach to erecting a natal horoscope chart. Give it no more concern.

AUXILIARY TECHNIQUES

The birthchart captures a single moment or slice of time. There are some other techniques that can be used in conjunction with the birthchart:

Transits: The birthchart can be compared to the current planetary positions. The resultant current date chart is called a TRANSIT CHART, which relates the astrological factors that exist in the sky now to those that existed at the moment of your birth. The birthchart shows innate birth patterns, powers, and potentials (i.e., basic nature). The transits show the current day-to-day development of the birth power (i.e., how that basic nature is revealing itself on any given day).

Progressions: Another popular technique is to relate the birthchart to that same birthchart that has been progressed into the future. The birthchart can be progressed to any future date because the movement of the planets in the sky is predictable. Astrologers have a wide variety of methods of progressing a chart. The "day-for-a-year" method is very popular. By this method, one day (24-hour revolution) is equated with one year (seasonal cycle) of life. Thus the 35th day after birth is considered to represent the 35th year after birth, and so on. A chart for the 35th day after birth is calculated and compared to the natal chart. A progressed chart shows future possibilities and probabilities and gives powerful clues as to how the future can best be used.

Returns: Another popular method is that of SOLAR RETURNS and LUNAR RETURNS. In this technique, a chart is calculated for the precise time that the Sun (or Moon) returns to the position it had at your birth. Thus if your Natal Sun was at 25 degrees and 48 minutes of the Sign Cancer, a Solar Return chart would be one cast for the Sun's return to this identical spot during the current year. This chart is then compared to the birthchart. I briefly mention it here to make you aware of the terms and because it is part of the big picture of natal astrology.

This has been a very general introduction to some of the basic terms and processes used in astrology. As a beginner in astrology, a simple birthchart and interpretation is probably all you will need. In the future, you may want more complete interpretations dealing with your year ahead or perhaps a comparison report between yourself and some other person to see how compatible (or incompatible) you are. Or perhaps you will be inspired to study on your own and become more advanced or even become a professional astrologer. Elsewhere in this book I will recommend various books to help further your study if that is your desire. Those books, in turn, will lead to even more advanced study. And so it goes.

Astrology has such a broad scope and has so many facets to it, that there is something to satisfy everyone's specific needs and desires.

THE PHILOSOPHY OF ASTROLOGY

I'll now briefly explain what astrology is and what it is not in simple, non-technical language. I'll discuss what astrological counseling is and how you can use this powerful tool to your advantage. There are many different types of astrology, each with its own special purpose. This booklet is confined to natal astrology. Natal astrology deals with the birth-patterning of individuals.

Astrology is just one of many tools we have at our disposal to help us deal with problems and enrich our lives. Some other tools are: self-hypnosis; meditation; prayer; education. Like all tools, astrology gets the job done when it is understood and used properly.

What natal astrology is:

1. A tool that provides greater understanding of yourself.

2. The oldest empirical science in the world.

3. A patterning of a person's innate birth potentials, strengths, weaknesses, tendencies, and probabilities. Intelligent information is available on every aspect of a person's life from cradle to grave.

What natal astrology is *not*:

1. It is *not* a cure-all.

2. It is *not* fatalistic. The individual always has the ability to choose by exercising the birthright of free will.

3. It does *not* advocate that the planets control our lives. We, through our choices, control our own lives.

I do not personally know any astrologer who thinks that planets cause events in our lives.

We astrologers believe in the oneness of the universe and in the dependence, interdependence, interaction, and mutual reflectiveness of everything.

Astrology is based on the observation that events here on Earth are instantly reflected in the heavens. A simplistic analogy might be this: If you look into a mirror while trimming your eyebrows and you accidentally pierce your skin with the scissors, you will instantly see the wound bleeding in the mirror. The mirror did not cause the wound or the bleeding, did it? The mirror accurately reflected an event at the precise time the event occurred.

If it were possible to have a mirror that looked ahead in time, you could have seen the accident ahead of time and thus avoid it by exercising more care or by not trimming your eyebrows at that time.

In astrology, the heavens (the planetary positions and movements), are our mirror of earthly events. Nearly five thousand years of careful observation and record-keeping have supplied us with accurate knowledge as to what kinds of earthly events are associated with what kinds of heavenly patterns.

Our astrological mirror is superior to our bathroom mirror because the planets' patterning is constantly changing. The planets and their relationships to each other, and to the Earth, change unendingly in a predictable way. We can calculate exactly where every planet will be at any time in relationship to any location on Earth. This means we have a mirror that can reflect events in the past, present, or future anywhere on Earth. An awesome thought, is it not?

This powerful tool was given to us as part of creation. The planets were created as part of our world for our use. The science of astrology strives to understand and use this great gift for the benefit of humanity.

Even though it is about five-thousand-years old, astrology is still in its infancy. The planet Pluto, for instance, was only discovered in February 1930, and it is still being studied. Who knows what might be out there to provide us with even more information?

Still, a great deal of valuable, useful information is known and can be used to enrich our lives and help us to make better decisions and choices.

It works this way. Suppose your birth occurred at 6:44 PM EST, on March 31, 1960, in Kingston, New York. The astrologers calculates the position of the Sun, Moon, and the eight known planets at that moment with respect to that specific geographic location on earth. He/she determines that your natal Sun is at 11 degrees and 15 minutes of Aries in your 6th house; your Moon is at 5 degrees and 7 minutes of Gemini in your 8th house; and so forth for the remaining eight known planets.

The astrologer then enters the information onto a circular map (such as shown in Figure One) known as a birthchart, which shows your unique birth patterning. He/she then studies the hundreds of factors in the patterning and compiles the data into a report known as your natal horoscope analysis. This report can tell virtually everything about all aspects of your life as reflected at your birth moment in the mirror of the heavens.

This kind of natal horoscope report can be greatly beneficial. Suppose, for example, you are unsure of a career path to pursue. Your chart will tell you in which pursuits you have the best chance of being successful and then you can make a choice based on this knowledge rather than just shooting blindly in the dark.

Predictive astrology is similar to natal astrology except that predictive astrology looks at a future date and analyzes your options at that time. This knowledge can help you avoid or lessen problems and take better advantage of opportunities.

What can astrology do to enhance a person's life? Let's examine three of the most dominant factors in the life of a person: companionship; career; and time.

Companionship: An astrologer can do a compatibility analysis between any two people and very accurately delineate the positive and negative aspects of a given relationship. The axiom "forewarned is half armed" applies here. The more you know about the compatibility (or incompatibility) between you and another person, the better equipped you are to interact with that person to your benefit.

I did a compatibility analysis for a young lady who was going to marry a man she was certain she deeply loved. Their birthcharts showed that the mutual attraction was totally physical, very strongly so, and that they had virtually nothing else in common. In addition, his chart showed a violent temper and a sadistic nature. In spite of this, she chose to marry him. Within a few weeks after the marriage, he beat her brutally. Fortunately, she remembered my warning and left him before he could hurt her further. Astrology clearly showed her the probabilities and choices, but the choice was hers alone to make.

One can wisely use this feature of astrology to improve chances of having a harmonious and happy relationship. Relationship applies not only to marriage, but also to romance, friendship, business, or any sort of partnership.

But in any situation, it is the individual's choice that directs the events, not the planets'. The planets show the parameters involved and the likely result of choices. But always, the individual's choice prevails. This is the least understood, and most important, factor in astrology. Astrology is not fatalistic. The individual is in charge. The birthchart shows the potentials; the individual makes the choices.

Career: I have already mentioned briefly that your chart can identify your innate talents, strengths, and abilities. Often a person selects a career path because of money, family tradition, or just by chance. Rarely do these careers produce self-fulfillment. How much better it would be to select a career that takes advantage of what you have to offer and of your interests.

I did an analysis for a thirty-eight-year-old bachelor. He was grossly unhappy with every aspect of his life. His chart showed why. He was a mediocre, bored electronics engineer, yet his chart very strongly indicated that law enforcement was his strongest interest and latent talent. He readily admitted that he had always wanted to be a policeman since he was a young boy. But peer and parental pressure to select a career that paid well influenced him to become an engineer. His chart showed a slight ability for engineering, hence he could do it, but it wasn't even close to being his strong suit. In addition, his chart indicated a strong materialistic streak. It also showed a love of children and a desire for marriage. He chose to let materialism dominate him; as a result he drove women away rather than attracting them. If he had had his birthchart done years earlier, he would have clearly seen his probabilities and options and might have made some different choices to ensure his happiness.

Time: Many people burn up time in unproductive pursuits just to keep busy and kill excess time. Others pine away their time in loneliness. Neither situation has to be that way. Everyone is so multi-faceted in talent and interests that there is plenty of self-fulfilling activity in which to engage. Most people do not realize this truth. They go through life in a one-dimensional fashion because they haven't discovered their multi-dimensional nature. A birthchart and analysis will clearly show each person's depth, talents, abilities, etc. Armed with this knowledge, it becomes easy to select extracurricular activities that are fulfilling and worthwhile, be it a hobby, avocation, second career, volunteer work, travel, or whatever. Again astrology presents the options—you make the choice. Some may choose to become amateur astrologers. This will eat up as much time as you choose to devote, and it is an excellent way to get to know, understand, and meet people.

There is nothing magical about this process. It is all based on fact, calculations, and interpretation by a qualified person. The skill of the astrologer is the only weak link in the chain. A good astrologer will erect an accurate chart and interpret it accurately. An unskilled or careless astrologer will not do a good job. But this isn't unique to astrology, is it? The same is true of all professions. A good physician helps you get well while a poor one just drains your money or causes additional problems. A competent mechanic makes your car run properly, an incompetent one doesn't.

The point is that astrology is a viable science that can be of value in your life. It merits your open-minded consideration.

Astrology does not have all the answers and is not a cure-all. It is just one of many tools available for you to use in order to better orchestrate the direction of your life. It is not fatalistic. In all cases, astrology presents your options. The choice you make is always up to you alone. You alone are the captain of your ship. Astrology merely provides a more complete map for you to set sail with.

Your map is your birthchart, which contains the powerful information you need to make the best choices in every aspect of your life so your life will be what you want it to be. This is raw, undiluted power!

Now let us take a more detailed look at what your birthchart can tell you.

ANALYSIS FACTORS IN BIRTHCHARTS

The power contained in your birthchart is in a coded form which must be decoded in order to glean the information. The factors that must be analyzed (decoded) are many, but it can be learned by an average person with a little help from a book such as *Astrology for Beginners*.

The primary factors involved in a birthchart are:

- What specific zodiacal Sign appears on the cusp of each house?

- What specific zodiacal Sign is each planet in? The Sun and Moon are considered to be planets in the analysis although technically they are luminaries, not planets. Their influence in the chart is the same as that of a planet.

- In which houses do the planets appear?

- Which specific degree of the Zodiac appears on each house cusp and on each planet placement? There are a total of 360 degrees in the Zodiac, and each degree has a specific influence.

- What is the specific relationship (in degrees) between each planet and each other planet? And what is the relationship (in degrees) between each planet and the Ascendant (1st house cusp) and the Midheaven (10th house cusp)? These relationships are called aspects.

- There are other factors also such as Arabian Parts, midpoints, declinations, and more.

For most people, especially beginners, only the zodiacal Signs, houses, planets, and aspects need to be considered in order to determine the basic power in the birthchart.

Let's take a broad look at the four major factors in birthchart analysis.

Zodiac Signs: These are also called Sun Signs and they are the most significant factor in a birthchart. Because of their importance, I have included a mini-profile of each of the Sun Signs a little later in this booklet.

Houses: Every possible aspect of a person's life is ruled by one of the houses. Therefore, the 12 houses of a birthchart depict the entire life of the person in every respect.

The complete list of everything each house rules is much too long to be given in this small booklet. To give you an inkling of each house rulership, the following list gives just one or two items of the many dozens of items ruled by each house.

1st:	Personality
2nd:	Self-earned money, values
3rd:	Communications, siblings
4th:	Home life
5th:	Love affairs and children
6th:	Job environment
7th:	Marriage
8th:	Death, transformation
9th:	Philosophy, travel
10th:	Career

11th: Friends, organizations
12th: Unconscious, psychism

Planets: Each of the planets has its own unique basic characteristics that it carries with it regardless of which house or in which Sign it appears.

Of course, the action of each planet varies because its influence blends with, and is influenced by, the action of its respective Sign and house. The aspects a planet makes with other planets are also a modifying influence.

However, the basic characteristics of each planet will be strong enough to be apparent in every birthchart regardless of these influences.

Each planet has many dozens of salient characteristics, far too many to be enumerated here. For a tiny sampling, here is just one of the many characteristics of each planet.

Sun:	Ego
Moon:	Creativity
Mercury:	Awareness
Venus:	Love
Mars:	Energy
Jupiter:	Good fortune
Saturn:	Patience
Uranus:	Unexpected events
Neptune:	Mystic experiences
Pluto:	Secrets

Aspects: The relationships between planets in a birthchart are called aspects. Because of space constraints, I will cover only the major aspects, and only in the briefest way in order to give you some appreciation of how the power in a birthchart is established.

Conjunction is when two planets are within 8 degrees of each other. This aspect intensifies the power of each of the planets involved, elevating them to more prominence in the birthchart.

Trine is when two planets are within 112 to 128 degrees apart. This aspect brings a strong element of good fortune to the affairs of the planets involved.

Sextile is when two planets are within 54 to 66 degrees apart. This aspect brings a strong element of opportunity to the affairs of the planets involved.

Square is when two planets are within 82 to 98 degrees apart. This aspect brings a strong element of obstacles to the affairs of the planets involved.

Opposition is when two planets are within 172 to 188 degrees apart. This aspect brings a strong element of "pushing and pulling" in one's life with regard to the affairs of the planets involved.

SOME EXAMPLES

Using Figure One as an example, here is just one of hundreds of factors that the chart shows, indicating a part of the power in that chart.

My Mercury (ME) is placed in the Sign Gemini (GE) in the 10th house. One of the things governed by the 10th house is career; the 10th house is also a public house and is one of the four most powerful houses in a birthchart. One of the things governed by Mercury is writers. Mercury is especially powerful because it is in the zodiacal Sign that it rules (Gemini). Gemini rules, among other things, communications of all sorts and writers. This indicates that one of the most powerful birth gifts I have is to be a writer for the public. That is exactly what my career is: I write books, articles, stories, and technical material for the public.

If I had had this knowledge when I was a young man, I could have groomed myself for this career at an earlier age without having to spend my time floundering around in life doing many other things for which I had some minor ability. In other words, I could have capitalized on the power in my birthchart. Instead, I finally learned about the power in my birthchart when I was in my mid-forties. As soon as I learned of this power, I concentrated on it and quickly became a successful writer. I was a late bloomer. I could have been an early bloomer if I had known the complete story of my potentials.

I mentioned earlier that it is possible to look into the future using a progressed birthchart. Here is one small example from my own birthchart.

My natal Sun is in Cancer at 12 degrees and 5 minutes (refer to Figure One). In a progressed birthchart, the Sun advances one degree for each year after birth. Therefore, when I reached 18 years of age, my progressed Sun reached zero degrees Leo (12 degrees Cancer + 18 years = 30 degrees; the thirtieth degree is zero degrees of the next sign).

The significance of this is: As a typical Cancer, I was extremely shy, timid, and introverted. The sign Leo is just the opposite, being outgoing and dramatic. At age 18 I decided I needed to change in order to succeed. I entered the Air Force, rose quickly in rank where I was forced to be outgoing, commanding, and dramatic, fulfilling the demands that a progressed Leo Sun was making on me. Subsequently I have become a business executive, lecturer, and public figure (through my writing) which would have been completely out of character for my timid, Cancer nature.

After learning astrology I have been able to accurately foresee upcoming changes in my life and thus be prepared for the change. For example, I accurately predicted to the exact day when I would be laid off from one job I had. As a result, I wasn't shocked. Instead I planned, and took, a three-month vacation in my motor home because I also foresaw that my potential for quickly getting another job was poor at that time, but the chance would improve significantly in about three to four months. So my wife and I had a great vacation touring much of the United States, and when we returned I located another job almost immediately. The power of my birthchart has aided me literally hundreds of times in enhancing the quality of my life.

In your own birthchart, if you analyze every planet, sign, house placement, and aspect, you will have an excellent knowledge of every facet of your life. If you want your life to bloom for you on all fronts, get started now. Do not delay further. Obtain your birthchart and learn of all your potentials and powers. Once you know, there is nothing to hold you back unless you refuse to take action.

A RE-CAP

Earlier I posed the question, "What is a birthchart and how do we use it?" We have answered that question by discussing the big picture, philosophy, giving examples, and giving some salient technical information about astrology.

There is no intent here to teach you astrology beyond a pre-beginner level. To learn more, you will need to read more comprehensive books on astrology such as the ones I have recommended in the Appendix.

At this point, the following factors are covered:

1. Your birthchart contains the information you need to know in order to realize the power you were given at birth.

2. You owe it to yourself to discover the power in your birthchart so that you can take full advantage of your birth power.

3. Your birthchart is a map to help you direct your journey through life to your best advantage.

To give you some basic information to help you begin to understand yourself and others, I am including mini-profiles of the Sun Signs.

SUN SIGN MINI-PROFILES

The cornerstone of birthchart interpretation is the Sun Sign profile of each of the twelve zodiacal Signs. There are a great number of other factors that are important also such as planet placements, houses, Midheaven, Ascendant, degrees, aspects, etc. But it all starts with the Sun Sign profile. Having some knowledge of all Sun Signs is necessary whether you are analyzing a chart or simply trying to better understand yourself or others.

The mini-profiles that follow are certainly not all-inclusive, but they do cover some salient points and provide you with a little knowledge of each Sign.

I am spending only a page or so on each Sun Sign, just touching on some characteristics. This will give you information that will enable you to talk knowledgeably, begin to understand a little of the power in your birthchart, and have a good time.

When any given Sign is on a house cusp, or any planet is in a given Sign, that house or planet will be influenced by the properties of the Sign.

ARIES

Aries is the first Sign of the Zodiac, and the ruling planet is Mars. Arian people are action-oriented and competitive, striving to be first in everything— often to the point of ignoring the rights and feelings of others. If they can learn to temper their aggressiveness with tact they can accomplish much. They are natural leaders. They like to start things, leaving it to others to finish, because they want to move on to some new challenge.

Some of Aries' characteristics are: dynamic, impulsive, quarrelsome, easily bored, selfish, enthusiastic, forceful. Interests are: themselves, challenges, starting things. They have a basic pioneer nature. They also tend to be warlike.

Aries have great willpower and confidence in themselves. If they can learn to love and respect others and to act with wisdom there is virtually no limit to their accomplishments. They never admit defeat. They will keep on fighting and striving until they either succeed or death overtakes them. They ask no quarter, and give none.

We have had several United States presidents born under the Sign of Aries, among them Thomas Jefferson and John Tyler.

Aries are the pioneers of the Zodiac.

> Key Phrase: I AM!
> Key Word: Action
> Virtue: Courage
> Defect: Arrogance
> Ruling Planet: Mars

TAURUS

Taurus is the second Sign of the Zodiac, ruled by the planet Venus. Taurus people like the good things in life and usually focus their energies on acquiring material possessions and money. They zestfully pursue everything that will satisfy their desires—this can be pleasure, comfort, or wealth.

Taurus people appreciate beautiful things whether it be art, music, or nice clothing. They are very stable people and are reliable, although usually quite stubborn.

Some Taurus characteristics are: materialistic; lazy; somewhat slow, but always finish what they start; patient; practical; steady; endurance. Interests are: comfort, possessions of all sorts. These people are fiercely loyal to their friends, burdening themselves with their friends' problems although they also can be very jealous. Taureans tend to not be too aware of themselves or their motives. They are great planners and hard workers.

We have had several United States presidents born under the Sign of Taurus, among them Harry S. Truman and Ulysses S. Grant.

Taurus people are the accumulators and builders of the Zodiac.

> Key Phrase: I HAVE!
> Key Word: Possessions
> Virtue: Reliability
> Defect: Stubbornness
> Ruling Planet: Venus

GEMINI

Gemini is the third Sign of the Zodiac and is ruled by the planet Mercury, the planet of mentality and communication. Geminis are probably the most intelligent people of the Zodiac. They have quick minds and are curious about virtually everything. The only problem is that they rarely have any self discipline. Therefore, they lack the staying power to finish what they start. They are the "Jack-of-all-trades, and master of none." If a Gemini acquires self-discipline there is nothing he/she cannot achieve.

Geminis are happiest when they are involved in many pursuits at the same time. They prefer intellectual activities such as philosophy, writing, talking, or thinking up things for others to do. They need to cultivate calmness because they are in danger of "burnout" as a result of nervous stress.

Some Gemini characteristics are: fickleness, superficial, witty, inquisitive, intelligent, versatile. Interests are: communication of all sorts, travel, knowing it all, learning, talking, writing, reading.

One United States president, John F. Kennedy, was born under the Sign of Gemini.

Geminis are the salespersons and communicators of the Zodiac. They are also the nonconformists of the Zodiac.

> Key Phrase: I THINK!
> Key Word: Variety
> Virtue: Alertness
> Defect: Shallowness
> Ruling Planet: Mercury

CANCER

Cancer is the fourth Sign of the Zodiac and is ruled by the Moon. Cancer people are very sensitive and emotional. Home and family life are of the utmost importance to them as is domestic security.

Cancer people are easily hurt by the slights of others. They are complex, sometimes appearing strong and at other times very vulnerable. Very few people ever really grasp the nature of Cancers; therefore Cancer people never receive the necessary understanding from others.

Cancers are very loving—once a love is begun, they never stop loving. However, they can be very cruel enemies. They are shy, even timid, moody, and react more from intuition or emotion than from reason. They are masters of the art of passive resistance. They can be directed through kindness, but if forced, they become immovable. Some characteristics are: moody, domestic, family-oriented, sensitive, emotional, tenacious. Interests are: home, security, love of country.

We have had several United States presidents born under the Sign of Cancer, among them Calvin Coolidge and Gerald Ford.

Cancers are the homemakers of the Zodiac.

Key Phrase: I FEEL!
Key Word: Tenacity
Virtue: Caring
Defect: Combative
Ruling Planet: Moon

LEO

Leo is the fifth Sign of the Zodiac and is ruled by the Sun. These are noble and generous people, although they often possess oversized egos. They are over-confident, blunt, and outspoken. These characteristics often cause them to lose friends. Leos are courageous and loyal. They like to be in charge and especially enjoy being in the spotlight, or at least at the center of attention. Leos are strongly attracted to the opposite sex.

Some characteristics are: romantic, idealistic, ambitious, egotistical, temperamental, loyal, enthusiastic, generous, optimistic, domineering, affectionate. Interests are: sports and games, achievement, fun, being in the spotlight, children (especially theirs). Woe be unto anyone who hurts a Leo's child!

We have had several United States presidents born under the Sign of Leo, among them Herbert Hoover and Benjamin Harrison.

Leos are the entertainers (sometimes clowns) of the Zodiac. They are also the "ones in charge."

Key Phrase: I WILL!
Key Word: Power
Virtue: Magnanimous or noble
Defect: Ostentatious or show-offish
Ruling Planet: Sun

VIRGO

Virgo is the sixth Sign of the Zodiac, ruled by the planet Mercury. Virgos constantly search for knowledge. They are detail-conscious, practical, efficient, and do well in any line of work that requires exactness.

Sometimes they become so immersed in detail that they lose sight of the big picture. Excessive worry can adversely affect their health. If they learn to think positive thoughts, they usually have very good health and are also of great benefit to humanity. Virgos often are attracted to some branch of the medical profession.

Of all the signs, Virgos are most likely to remain unmarried because they have difficulty in finding anyone to fit their high standards. Characteristics are: methodical, neat, reliable, practical, mental, industrious, cautious. Interests are: work, details, perfection.

We have had several United States presidents born under the Sign of Virgo, among them William H. Taft and Lyndon B. Johnson.

Virgos are the craftspeople of the Zodiac.

Key Phrase: I ANALYZE!
Key Word: Service
Virtue: Thoroughness
Defect: Pettiness or fussiness
Ruling Planet: Mercury

LIBRA

Libra is the seventh Sign of the Zodiac and is ruled by Venus. Librans are rarely loners; they want and need companionship—marriage is very important to them. They prefer an occupation that brings them in partnership or close contact with others. They make good counselors and judges as they clearly see both sides of an issue. However, this ability frequently causes problems in decision-making, especially concerning minor matters.

Libras have a strong sense of justice and fair play. They rarely express anger, but when they do it is usually a storm which subsides quickly—they do not hold grudges as anger leaves them feeling ill.

Characteristics are: romantic, dependent, cooperative, gracious, somewhat materialistic. Interests are: peace, beauty, social life.

We have had several United States presidents born under the Sign of Libra, among them Dwight D. Eisenhower and James E. Carter.

Libras are the diplomats of the Zodiac.

Key Phrase: I BALANCE!
Key Word: Harmony
Virtue: Fairness
Defect: Indecisiveness
Ruling Planet: Venus

Note: There are two correct ways to pronounce Libra: "Lee-bra" or "lie-bra." "The "lee-bra" pronunciation is the one most often used. However, the "Lie-bra" pronunciation is the one commonly used by professional astrologers. So if you want to sound like a well-informed astrologer, say "lie-bra."

SCORPIO

Scorpio is the eighth Sign of the Zodiac, ruled by Pluto. Scorpios have strong will power and an intense emotional drive. Their sex-drive is usually very strong. They are not "half-way" people; whatever they do, they do it with intensity and completeness. They have no fear of death. They need high integrity to avoid undesirable traits such as violence, jealousy, hatred, or possessiveness.

These people often become workaholics. They drive themselves hard, and usually drive others unmercifully. They despise weakness in themselves or others.

Scorpios are secretive people. They also are ruthless enemies or competitors.

Some Scorpio characteristics are: vindictive, sarcastic, heroic, forceful, cynical, secretive, determined, suspicious. Interests are: sex, unraveling mysteries, other people's money, being an unseen power.

There have been more United States presidents born under the Sign of Scorpio than under any other Sign. Two of these are Theodore Roosevelt and John Adams.

Scorpios are the detectives of the Zodiac.

Key Phrase: I DESIRE!
Key Word: Resourcefulness
Virtue: Intense dedication
Defect: Vindictiveness
Ruling Planet: Pluto

SAGITTARIUS

Sagittarius is the ninth Sign of the Zodiac, ruled by Jupiter, the planet of expansiveness and good fortune. Sagittarians are honest and freedom-loving people. No matter how difficult a situation becomes, they always seem to be under some sort of protective shield for help invariably arrives.

These people call the shots as they see them —they are often considered to be blunt or lacking in tact. Sagittarian women make charming companions, but usually dislike domestic tasks and are generally quite independent.

These are idealistic people. They must learn wisdom and balance or else they can become fanatics and blindly follow some narrow dogma.

Some Sagittarians characteristics are: optimistic, friendly, argumentative, generally easy-going. Interests are: religion, philosophy, traveling (especially foreign), horses, law, books, publishing, giving advice.

We have had several United States presidents born under the Sign of Sagittarius, among them Zachary Taylor and Martin Van Buren.

Sagittarians are the philosophers of the Zodiac.

Key Phrase: I SEE!
Key Word: Freedom
Virtue: Hopefulness
Defect: Non-discriminating
Ruling Planet: Jupiter

CAPRICORN

Capricorn is the tenth Sign of the Zodiac, ruled by Saturn. These people are frugal, hard-working, and dedicated to achieving their goals. If they maintain integrity, they can achieve the highest of accomplishments. If they lack integrity, they may also achieve the highest accomplishments, but they assuredly will have the greatest of falls. This is because the ruling planet, Saturn, always gives perfect justice—what you sow, you will reap.

These are practical people. They will let nothing stand in their way. They are indefeatable enemies and loyal friends. They are neat and methodical. They also are frequently "slave drivers."

They do not function well for long in subordinate positions, needing to be in charge, even if in a small way. As a rule, they live to a ripe old age.

Characteristics are: serious, frugal, ambitious, realistic, cautious, responsible, worriers, hardworking. Interests are: business, material success, being in charge.

We have had several United States presidents born under the Sign of Capricorn, among them Andrew Johnson and Woodrow Wilson.

Capricorns are the organizers of the Zodiac.

Key Phrase: I USE!
Key Word: Ambition
Virtue: Respectfulness
Defect: Condescending
Ruling Planet: Saturn

AQUARIUS

Aquarius is the eleventh Sign of the Zodiac, ruled by Uranus. This is the sign of brotherhood and friendship. Aquarians are loyal friends.

These are tireless workers, and prefer to work in some endeavor that has humanitarian benefits. They have great desire for material gain, but are not greedy. They are willing to work for what they want, and do not demand more than their fair share. Because they take their work seriously, they are usually a bundle of nerves inside; this frequently can make them ill. However, to outward appearances, they seem to be calm.

With Aquarius, what you see is what you get—they do not put on facades or affectations. They have great dislike for hypocrisy. These are determined, stubborn, and often argumentative people with the ability to stir up much dislike toward themselves.

Characteristics are: tactless, independent, naive, broadminded, dogmatic, rebellious, impersonal. Interests are: helping others, friends, astrology, truth, politics.

We have had several United States presidents born under the Sign of Aquarius, among them Abraham Lincoln and Franklin D. Roosevelt.

Aquarians are the reformers of the Zodiac.

Key Phrase: I KNOW!
Key Word: Independence
Virtue: Friendliness
Defect: Eccentricity
Ruling Planet: Uranus

PISCES

Pisces is the twelfth Sign of the Zodiac, ruled by Neptune. These are very sensitive people, responsive to thoughts and feelings of others. They rarely participate in sports or strenuous activity. They will suffer rather than fight for their rights—they can have a martyr complex. They can be unreasonably stubborn. They also like to drift, rather than buckle down to responsibility.

They alternate between pessimism and optimism. In fact, much of their behavior goes from one extreme to the other, which is annoying to those around them. Generally, these are not ambitious people. They seem to be tuned-in to some dream world, often excelling in all fields of art. They have overactive imaginations. Pisceans are blind to faults in anyone they love.

Characteristics are: sensitive, impressionable, changeable, day-dreaming, compassionate, psychic, careless, dependent. Interests are: hospitals, medicine, pets, drugs, just thinking, serving others.

We have had several United States presidents born under the Sign of Pisces, among them George Washington and Andrew Jackson.

Pisces are the martyrs of the Zodiac.

Key Phrase I BELIEVE
Key Word: Compassion
Virtue: Charitableness
Defect: Easily influenced
Ruling Planet: Neptune

ONE FINAL THOUGHT

We are a blend of the influences of all the Sun Signs because our birthcharts contain all the zodiacal Signs on house cusps and have planets in some of the Signs.

That explains, for example, why I am a professional writer, which is a Gemini trait, even though I have a Cancer Sun Sign. In Figure One you can see that I have three planets (Jupiter, Moon, and Mercury) in Gemini in the powerful 10th house. I have more planets in Gemini than in any other sign. Plus the planet Mercury, which rules Gemini, is in Gemini, which greatly intensifies the Gemini influence over my career choice.

Thus you can see that knowing just your Sun Sign is not sufficient to understand your birth patterning. However, knowledge of all Sun Signs is the necessary place to start. Then add knowledge of individual planets, houses, and aspect influences, and you will have a complete picture of your birth patterning.

I recommend that you consider obtaining your birthchart and interpreting it or having it interpreted. Once you see first-hand the value of this, you will no doubt want to do the same for your loved ones and perhaps even for close associates.

APPENDIX

Astrology for Beginners by William W. Hewitt, Llewellyn Publications, 275 pages.

Learn the fundamentals of natal astrology. Learn what astrology is and what it can do for you. Create and interpret your birthchart. Explore transits, predictive astrology and progressions. Calculate, an accurate birthchart. Learn about references for more detailed material.

STAY IN TOUCH

On the following pages you will find some of the books now available on related subjects. Your book dealer stocks most of these and will stock new titles in the Llewellyn series as they become available. We urge your patronage.

To obtain our full catalog, to keep informed about new titles as they are released and to benefit from informative articles and helpful news, you are invited to write for our bimonthly news magazine/catalog, *Llewellyn's New Worlds of Mind and Spirit*. A sample copy is free, and it will continue coming to you at no cost as long as you are an active mail customer. Or you may subscribe for just $10.00 in the U.S.A. and Canada ($20.00 overseas, first class mail). Many bookstores also have *New Worlds* available to their customers. Ask for it.

Llewellyn's New Worlds of Mind and Spirit
P.O. Box 64383-351, St. Paul, MN 55164-0383, U.S.A.

* * *

TO ORDER BOOKS AND TAPES

If your book dealer does not have the books described, you may order them directly from the publisher by sending full price in U.S. funds, plus $3.00 for postage and handling for orders *under* $10.00; $4.00 for orders *over* $10.00. There are no postage and handling charges for orders over $50.00. Postage and handling rates are subject to change. We ship UPS whenever possible. Delivery guaranteed. Provide your street address as UPS does not deliver to P.O. Boxes. UPS to Canada requires a $50.00 minimum order. Allow 4-6 weeks for delivery. Orders outside the U.S.A. and Canada: Airmail—add retail price of book; add $5.00 for each non-book item (tapes, etc.); add $1.00 per item for surface mail.

LLEWELLYN PUBLICATIONS
P.O. Box 64383-351, St. Paul, MN 55164-0383, U.S.A.

COMPUTERIZED ASTROLOGY REPORTS

Simple Natal: Your chart calculated by computer in the Tropical/Placidus House system or the House system of your choice. It has all of the trimmings, including aspects, midpoints, Chiron and a glossary of symbols, plus a free booklet!

APS03-119 . . . .$5.00

Personality Profile Horoscope: Our most popular reading! This ten-part reading gives you a complete look at how the planets affect you. Learn about your general characteristics and life patterns. Look into your imagination and emotional needs. It is an excellent way to become acquainted with astrology and to learn about yourself. Very reasonable price!

APS03-503 . . . .$20.00

Transit Forecasts: These reports keep you abreast of positive trends and challenging periods. Transit Forecasts can be an invaluable aid for timing your actions and decision making. Reports begin the first day of the month you specify.

3-month Transit Forecast APS03-500 . . . . $12.00
6-month Transit Forecast APS03-501 . . . . $20.00
1-year Transit Forecast APS03-502 . . . . $25.00

Life Progressions: Discover what the future has in store for you! This incredible reading covers a year's time and is designed to complement the Personality Profile Reading. Progressions are a special system with which astrologers map how the "natal you" develops through specified periods of your present and future life, and with this report you can discover the "now you!"

APSO3-507 . . . .$20.00

Personal Relationship Reading: If you've just called it quits on one relationship and know you need to understand more about yourself before you test the waters again, then this is the report for you! This reading will tell you how you approach relationships in general, what kind of people you look for and what kind of people might rub you the wrong way. Important for anyone!

APS03-506 . . . . $20.00

Compatibility Profile: Find out if you really are compatible with your lover, spouse, friend or business partner! This is a great way of getting an in-depth look at your relationship with another person. Find out each person's approach to the relationship. Do you have the same goals? How well do you deal with arguments? Do you have the same values? This service includes planetary placements for both individuals, so send birth data for both and specify the type of relationship (i.e., friends, lovers, etc.). Order today!

APS03-504 . . . . $30.00

Ultimate Astro-Profile: This report has it all! Receive over 40 pages of fascinating, insightful and uncanny descriptions of your innermost qualities and talents. Read about your burn rate (thirst for change). Explore your personal patterns (from both the inside and outside). Examine the particular pattern of your Houses. The Astro-Profile doesn't repeat what you've already learned from other personality profiles, but considers the often neglected natal influence of the lunar nodes, plus much more!

APS03-505 . . . . $40.00

ASTROLOGY FOR BEGINNERS
An Easy Guide to Understanding & Interpreting Your Chart
William Hewitt

Anyone who is interested in astrology will enjoy *Astrology for Beginners*. This book makes astrology easy and exciting by presenting all of the basics in an orderly sequence while focusing on the natal chart. Llewellyn even includes a coupon for a free computerized natal chart so you can begin interpretations almost immediately without complicated mathematics.

Astrology for Beginners covers all of the basics. Learn exactly what astrology is and how it works. Explore signs, planets, houses and aspects. Learn how to interpret a birth chart. Discover the meaning of transits, predictive astrology and progressions. Determine your horoscope chart in minutes without using math.

Whether you want to practice astrology for a hobby or aspire to become a professional astrologer, *Astrology for Beginners* is the book you need to get started on the right track.

0-87542-307-8, 288 pgs., 5-1/4 x 8, softcover $7.95

THE INSTANT HOROSCOPE READER
Planets by Sign, House and Aspect
Julia Lupton Skalka

Find out what was written in the planets at your birth! Almost everyone enjoys reading the popular Sun sign horoscopes in newspapers and magazines; however, there is much more to astrology than knowing what your Sun sign is. How do you interpret your natal chart so that you know what it means to have Gemini on your 8th house cusp? What does astrology say about someone whose Sun is conjoined with natal Jupiter?

The Instant Horoscope Reader was written to answer such questions and to give beginners a fresh, thorough overview of the natal chart. Here you will find the meaning of the placement of the Sun, the Moon and each planet in the horoscope, including aspects between the natal planets, the meaning of the houses in the horoscope and house rulerships. Even if you have not had your chart cast, this book includes simple tables that enable you to locate the approximate planetary and house placements and figure the planetary aspects for your birthdate to give you unique perspectives about yourself and others.

ISBN: 1-56718-669-6, 6 x 9, 272 pp., illus.   **$14.95**

THE BOOK OF LOVERS
Men Who Excite Women, Women Who Excite Men
Carolyn Reynolds

What are you looking for in a lover or potential mate? If it's money, set your sights on a Pisces/Taurus. Is exercise and health food your passion? Then a Virgo/Cancer will share it with you.

Where do you find these people? They're all here, in *The Book of Lovers*. Astrologer Carolyn Reynolds introduces a new and accurate way to determine romantic compatibility through the use of Sun and Moon sign combinations. And best of all, you don't have to know a single thing about astrology to use this book!

Here you will find descriptions of every man and woman born between the years 1900 and 2000. To see whether that certain someone could be "the one," simply locate his or her birthdata in the chart and flip to the relevant pages to read about your person's strengths and weaknesses, sex appeal, personality and most importantly, how they will treat you!

0-87542-289-0, 464 pgs., 6 x 9, softcover $14.95

YOUR PLANETARY PERSONALITY
Everything You Need to Make Sense of Your Horoscope
Dennis Oakland

This book deepens the study of astrological interpretation for professional and beginning astrologers alike. Dennis Oakland's interpretations of the planets in the houses and signs are the result of years of study of psychology, sciences, symbolism, Eastern philosophy plus the study of birth charts from a psychotherapy group. Unlike the interpretations in other books, these emphasize the life processes involved and facilitate a greater understanding of the chart. Includes 100-year ephemeris.

Even if you now know *nothing* about astrology, Dennis Oakland's clear instructions will teach you how to construct a complete and accurate birth chart for anyone born between 1900 to 1999. After you have built your chart, he will lead you through the steps of reading it, giving you indepth interpretations of each of your planets. When done, you will have the satisfaction that comes from increased self-awareness *and* from being your *own* astrologer!

This book is also an excellent exploration for psychologists and psychiatrists who use astrology in their practices.

0-87542-594-1, 580 pgs., 7 x 10, softcover $19.95

SIGNS OF LOVE
Your Personal Guide to Romantic and
Sexual Compatibility
Jeraldine Saunders

Unlimited love power can be yours through an intimate knowledge of your horoscope, your numerical birth path, and other vitally important signs and signals that lead the way to loving relationships.

Now in an irresistible approach to the human heart, Jeraldine Saunders, a noted authority on the mystic arts, shows you how to look for love, how to find it, and how to be sure of it. With the aid of astrology, graphology, numerology, palmistry, and face reading, you will discover everything you need to know about your prospects with a given individual. You will learn the two enemies of love and how to eliminate them; the characteristics of all twelve zodiacal signs; the signs that are compatible with yours; the secrets behind your lover's facial features.

Signs of Love is the ultimate guide for gaining a better understanding of yourself and others in order to create a meaningful love life and attain lasting happiness.

0-87542-706-5, 320 pgs., 6 x 9, illus., softcover $6.99

HEAVEN KNOWS WHAT
Grant Lewi

What better way to begin the study of astrology than to actually do it while you learn. *Heaven Knows What* contains everything you need to cast and interpret complete natal charts without memorizing any symbols, without confusing calculations, and without previous experience or training. The tear-out horoscope blanks and special "aspect wheel" make it amazingly easy.

The author explains the influence of every natal Sun and Moon combination, and describes the effects of every major planetary aspect in language designed for the modern reader. His readable and witty interpretations are so relevant that even long-practicing astrologers gain new psychological insight into the characteristics of the signs and meanings of the aspects.

Grant Lewi is sometimes called the father of "do-it-yourself" astrology, and is considered by many to have been astrology's forerunner to the computer.

0-87542-444-9, 372 pgs., 6 x 9, tables, charts, $12.95

THE NEW A TO Z HOROSCOPE MAKER AND DELINEATOR
Llewellyn George

This book serves as a textbook, encyclopedia, self-study course, and extensive astrological dictionary all in one! More American astrologers have learned their craft from the NEW A TO Z than any other astrology book. First published in 1910, it is in every sense a complete course in astrology, giving beginners ALL the basic techniques and concepts they need to get off on the right foot. Plus it offers the more advanced astrologer an excellent dictionary and reference work for calculating and analyzing transits, progression, rectifications, and creating locality charts. This new edition has been revised to met the needs of the modern audience.

0-87542-264-0, 592 pgs., 6 x 9, softcover $12.95

OTHER COMPUTERIZED REPORTS

Numerology Report: Find out which numbers are right for you with this report. It uses an ancient form of numerology invented by Pythagoras to determine the significant numbers in your life. Using both your *full* birth name and date of birth, this report will accurately calculate those numbers which stand out as yours.

3-month Numerology Report APSO3-508 . . . . . . $12.00
6-month Numerology Report APSO3-509 . . . . . . $18.00
12-month Numerology Report APSO3-510 . . . . . $25.00

Lucky Lotto Report (State Lottery Report): This report will determine your luckiest sequence of numbers for each day based on specific planets, degrees and other indicators in your own chart. Provide your full birth data and middle name, and specify the parameters of your state's lottery: i.e., how many numbers you need in sequence (up to 10 numbers) as well as the highest possible numeral (up to #999). Indicate the month you want to start.

3-month Lucky Lotto Report APS03-512 . . . . $10.00
6-month Lucky Lotto Report APS03-513 . . . . $15.00
12-month Lucky Lotto Report APS03-514 . . . . . . $25.00

Biorhythm Report: Ever have one of those days when you have unlimited energy and everything is going your way? Then the next day you are feeling sluggish and awkward? These cycles are called biorhythms. This individual report will accurately map your daily biorhythms. Each important day is thoroughly discussed. With this valuable information, you can schedule important events with great success. This report is an invaluable source of information to help you plan your days to the fullest. Order today!

3-month Biorhythm Report APS03-515 . . . .$12.00
6-month Biorhythm Report APS03-516 . . . .$18.00
12-month Biorhythm Report APS03-517 . . . .$25.00